Citizens Dissent

*Security, Morality, and
Leadership in an Age of Terror*

Essays by
Wendell Berry
David James Duncan

a publication of The Orion Society

Citizens Dissent

by Wendell Berry and David James Duncan

ISBN 0-913098-62-0
Copyright © 2003 by The Orion Society

The Orion Society
187 Main Street, Great Barrington, MA 01230
telephone: 413/528-4422   facsimile: 413/528-0676
email: orion@orionsociety.org   website: www.oriononline.org

Cover image: Detail of Robert Van Vranken's painting
Untitled (Myself if I am Real), 2001. Oil and mixed
media on plaster on board, 65x43x2.5 inches.
Courtesy of O.K. Harris Works of Art, New York, NY.

Designed by Jason Houston

Printed on New Leaf Reincarnation Matte paper.
100% recycled, 50% post-consumer, process chlorine free.
Printed in the U.S.A. by Excelsior Printing Co.

1st printing

Citizens Dissent

Foreword

Let every man make known what kind of government would com-
mand his respect, and that will be one step toward obtaining it.

From "On the Duty of Civil Disobedience"

—Henry David Thoreau

In the first two volumes of The Orion Society's New
Patriotism Series—*In the Presence of Fear* and *Patriotism
and the American Land*—the authors discuss the world as
it has changed since the September 11 tragedies from a
different perspective than that exhibited in much of the
media and political leadership. The intention of these
writers has been to show that it is impossible to see this
"new reality," this Age of Terror, without studying the
relationship between different kinds of terror, and without expanding our universe of concern.

This third volume is published at the same moment
that our nation's leadership, consistent with its promulgat-
ed *National Security Strategy of the United States of America*,
executes a war in Iraq. Following this new policy, our
Administration determined without specific congression-

al or voter approval that "we" must rid the world of an Iraqi regime, and in doing so must subject untold numbers of innocent civilians to death. These actions, these deaths, and future ones that are inevitable if the new National Security Strategy is followed, will be carried out in our names, as citizens of a two-century-old democratic republic. For those who choose to oppose these actions, for those who choose to oppose the worldview that generates them, the primary course of action is patriotic dissent—the essence of a true democracy.

Wendell Berry's "A Citizen's Response to the National Security Strategy of the United States of America" and David James Duncan's "When Compassion Becomes Dissent" are two such citizens' dissents. These two essays offer powerful meditations on issues of security and morality in an age of terror, and challenge the meaning and workings of democracy. Furthermore, both essays move far beyond a simplistic evaluation of sanctions and acts of war to present a viable model of leadership based on an enlightened understanding of the threats to and responsibilities of freedom.

Mr. Berry's "A Citizen's Response," placed in abridged form as a full-page statement in *The New York Times* on February 9, 2003 and seen by 1.7 million readers, draws attention to the numerous flaws and contradictions inherent in the new National Security Strategy, and urges us to expand the context with which we deal with questions of terror and security.

In a manner both informative and emotionally crushing, Mr. Duncan's "When Compassion Becomes Dissent" takes the literature of political dissent to a new place, where our values as individuals and as a nation are weighed not only against the facts of past and present misdeeds, but also against the vivid and palpable human toll that our now dominant worldview realizes on the innocent. His essay is not simply a work of conscience, but, like Thoreau's essay on civil disobedience, it is a haunting call to the collective conscience of the citizenry. And while the content and implications of his dissent are a very heavy burden for our souls to bear, his solution to what ails us begins with a very simple act— opening our hearts to a truth that, despite subtle and not so subtle attempts to obscure or redefine it, remains insoluble and unchanging.

The September 11 tragedies require of us the creation of a new world order. The National Security Strategy represents our Administration's attempt to forge a new world order through the preemptive use of military might against nations we deem evil. This third volume of The Orion Society's New Patriotism Series addresses that worldview, and offers a substantially different vision for our nation's policy and leadership in this defining moment of world history.

Marion Gilliam
Chairman

Laurie Lane-Zucker
Executive Director
& Series Editor

A Citizen's Response to the National Security Strategy of the United States of America

by Wendell Berry

I. The new National Security Strategy published by the White House in September 2002, if carried out, would amount to a radical revision of the political character of our nation. This document was conceived in reaction to the terrorist attacks of September 11, 2001. Its central and most significant statement is this:

> While the United States will constantly strive to enlist the support of the international community, we will not hesitate to act alone, if necessary, to exercise our right of self-defense by acting preemptively against such terrorists... (p. 6)

A democratic citizen must deal here first of all with the question, Who is this "we"? It is not the "we" of the

Declaration of Independence, which referred to a small group of signatories bound by the conviction that "governments [derive] their just powers from the consent of the governed." And it is not the "we" of the Constitution, which refers to "*the people* [my emphasis] of the United States."

Because of what is implied by the commitment to act alone and preemptively, this "we" of the new strategy can refer only to the president. It is a royal "we." A head of state, preparing to act alone in starting a preemptive war, will need to justify his intention by secret information, and will need to plan in secret and execute his plan without forewarning. A preemptive attack widely known and discussed, as in a democratic polity, would risk being preempted by a preemptive attack by the other side. The idea of a government acting alone in preemptive war is inherently undemocratic, for it does not require or even permit the president to obtain the consent of the governed. As a policy, this new strategy depends on the acquiescence of a public kept fearful and ignorant, subject to manipulation by the executive power, and on the compliance of an intimidated and office-dependent legislature. Even within the narrow logic of warfare, there is a substantial difference between a defensive action, for which the reason would be publicly known, and a preemptive or aggressive action, for which the reason would be known only by a few at the center of power. The responsibilities of the president obviously are not mine, and so I hesitate to doubt absolutely the necessity of governmental secrecy. But I feel no hesitation in saying that, to the extent that a government is secret, it cannot be democratic or its people free. By this new doctrine, the president alone may start a war against any nation at any time, and with no more forewarning than preceded the Japanese attack on Pearl Harbor.

Would-be participating citizens of a democratic nation, unwilling to have this issue of consent either ignored or coerced, therefore have no choice but to remove themselves from the illegitimate constraints of this "we" in as immediate and public a way as possible.

But as this document and its supporters insist, we have now entered a new era when acts of war may be carried out not only by nations and "rogue nations," but also by individuals using weapons of mass destruction, and this requires us to give up some measure of freedom in return for some increase of security. The lives of every one of us may at any time be in jeopardy.

Even so, we need to ask, What does real security require of us? What does true patriotism require of us? What does freedom require of us?

The alleged justification for this new strategy is the recent emergence in the United States of international terrorism. But why the events of September 11, 2001, horrifying as they were, should have called for a radical new investiture of power in the executive branch is not clear.

The National Security Strategy defines terrorism as "premeditated, politically motivated violence perpetrated against innocents" (p. 5). This is truly a distinct kind of violence, but it is a kind old and familiar, even in the United States. All that was really new about the events of September 11, 2001, was that they raised the scale of such violence to that of "legitimate" modern warfare.

To imply by the word "terrorism" that this sort of terror is the work exclusively of "terrorists" is misleading. The "legitimate" warfare of technologically advanced nations likewise is premeditated, politically motivated violence perpetrated against innocents. The distinction between the intention to perpetrate violence against innocents, as in "terrorism," and the willingness to do so, as in "war," is not a source of much comfort. We know also that modern war, like ancient war, often involves intentional violence against innocents.

A more correct definition of "terrorism" would be this: violence perpetrated unexpectedly without the authorization of a national government. Violence perpetrated unexpectedly with such authorization is not "terrorism" but "war." If a nation perpetrates violence officially—whether to bomb an enemy airfield or a hospital—it is not guilty of "terrorism." But there is no need to hesitate over the difference between "terrorism" and any violence or threat of violence that is terrifying. The National Security Strategy wishes to cause "terrorism" to be seen "in the same light as slavery, piracy, or genocide" (p. 6)—but not in the same light as war. It accepts and affirms the legitimacy of war.

This document concedes that "we are menaced less by

fleets and armies than by catastrophic technologies in the hands of the embittered few" (p. 1). And yet we continue to manufacture, stockpile, and trade in these catastrophic technologies, including nuclear, chemical, and biological weapons. In nuclear or biological warfare, in which we know we cannot limit effects, how do we distinguish our enemies from our friends—or our enemies from ourselves? Does this not bring us exactly to the madness of terrorists who kill themselves in order to kill others?

The official definition of "terrorism," then, is far too exclusive if we seriously wish to free the world of the terrors induced by human violence. But let us suppose that our opposition to terror could be justly or wisely limited to a "war against terrorism." How effective might such a war be?

The war against terrorism is not, strictly speaking, a war against nations, even though it has already involved international war in Afghanistan and presidential threats against other nations. This is a war against "the embit tered few"—"thousands of trained terrorists"—who, like drug dealers, are "at large" (p. 5) among many thousands and even millions of others who are, in the language of this document, "innocents," and thus are deserving of our protection.

Hunting these terrorists down will be like combing lice out of a head of hair. Unless we are willing to kill innocents in order to kill the guilty—unless we are will-ing to blow our neighbor's head off, or blow our own head off, to get rid of the lice—the need to be lethal will be impeded constantly by the need to be careful. Because of the inherent difficulties and because we must suppose a new supply of villains to be always in the making, we can expect the war on terrorism, like the war on drugs, to be more or less endless, endlessly costly and endlessly supportive of a thriving bureaucracy.

Unless, that is, we should become willing to ask why, and to do something about the causes. Why do people produce, market, and consume illegal drugs? Why do people become terrorists? Such questions are often dismissed as evidence of "liberal softness" toward malefactors. But that is not necessarily the case. Such questions may also arise from the recognition that problems have causes. There is, however, no acknowledgement in the National Security Strategy that terrorism might have a cause that could possibly be discovered and possibly remedied. "The embittered few," it seems, are merely "evil."

II. Much of the obscurity of our effort so far against terrorism originates in the now official idea that the enemy is evil and that we are (therefore) good, which is the precise mirror image of the official idea of the terrorists.

Each of the eleven parts of the National Security Strategy begins with a quotation from one of President Bush's speeches. The epigraph of Part III contains this sentence from his speech at the National Cathedral on September 14, 2001: "But our responsibility to history is already clear: to answer these attacks and rid the world of evil." A government, committing its nation to rid the world of evil, is assuming necessarily that it and its nation are good.

But the proposition that anything so multiple and large as a nation, or even a government, can be "good" is an insult to common sense. It is also dangerous, because it precludes any attempt at self-criticism or self-correction; it precludes public dialogue. It leads us far indeed from the traditions of religion and democracy that are intended to measure and so to sustain our efforts to be good. "There is none good but one, that is, God," Christ said. Also: "He that is without sin among you, let him first cast a stone at her." Can it be that Mr. Bush, a professed Christian, has forgotten? And Thomas Jefferson justified general education by the obligation of citizens to be critical of their government: "for nothing can keep it right but their own vigilant *and distrustful* [my emphasis] superintendence." An inescapable requirement of true patriotism, love for one's land, is a vigilant distrust of any determinative power, elected or unelected, that may preside over it.

And so it is not without reason or precedent that a would-be participating citizen should point out that, in addition to evils originating abroad and supposedly correctable by catastrophic technologies in "legitimate" hands, we have an agenda of domestic evils, not only those that properly self-aware humans can find in their own hearts, but also several that are indigenous to our history as a nation: issues of economic and social justice, and issues related to the continuing and worsening maladjustment between our economy and our land.

There are kinds of violence that have nothing directly to do with unofficial or official warfare, but are accepted as normal to our economic life. I mean such things as toxic pollution, land destruction, soil erosion, the destruction of biological diversity and of the ecological supports of agriculture. To anybody with a normal concern for health and sanity, these "externalized costs" are terrible and are terrifying.

I don't wish to make light of the threats and dangers that now confront us. There can be no doubt of the reality of terrorism as defined and understood by the National Security Strategy, or of the seriousness of our situation, or of our need for security. But frightening as this is, it does not relieve us of the responsibility to be as intelligent, principled, and practical as we can be. To rouse the public's anxiety about foreign terror while ignoring domestic terror, and to fail to ask if these terrors are in any way related, is wrong.

It is understandable that we should have reacted to the attacks of September 11, 2001, by reorganizing the national police, by curtailment of civil rights, by defiance of laws, and by resort to overwhelming force, for those things are relatively simple and are the ready products of fear and hasty thought. But they cannot protect us against the destruction of our own land by ourselves. They cannot protect us against the selfishness, silliness, and greed that we have legitimized here as economic virtues, and have taught to the world. They cannot protect us against our government's long-standing disdain for any form of national or regional self-sufficiency and for any form of thrift, or against the consequent dependence, which for the present at least is inescapable, on foreign supplies, such as oil from the Middle East.

And they cannot protect us from what may potentially be the greatest threat of all, the estrangement of our people from one another and from our land. Increasingly, Americans—including, notoriously, their politicians—are not from anywhere. And so they have in this "homeland," which their government now seeks to make secure on their behalf, no home place that they are strongly moved to know or love or use well or protect.

It is no wonder that the National Security Strategy, growing as it does out of unresolved contradictions in our domestic life, should attempt to compound a foreign policy out of contradictory principles.

There is, first of all, the contradiction of peace and war, or of war as the means of achieving and preserving peace. This document affirms peace, and it affirms peace as the justification of war and war as the means of peace—and thus perpetuates a hallowed absurdity. But implicit in its assertion of this (and, by implication, any other) nation's right to act alone in its own interest is an acceptance of war as a permanent condition. Either way, it is cynical to invoke the ideas of cooperation, community, peace, freedom, justice, dignity, and the rule of law (as this document repeatedly does), and then proceed to assert one's intention to act alone in making war. One cannot reduce terror by holding over the world the threat of what it most fears.

This is a contradiction not reconcilable except by a self-righteousness almost inconceivably naïve. The authors write that "We will...use our foreign aid to promote freedom and support those who struggle *non-violently* [my emphasis] for it" (p. 4); and they observe, on page 27, that

> In pursuing advanced military capabilities that can threaten its neighbors...China is following an outdated path that, in the end, will hamper its own pursuit of national greatness. In time, China will find that social and political freedom is the only source of that greatness.

Thus we come to the authors' implicit definition of "rogue state:" Any nation pursuing national greatness by advanced military capabilities that can threaten its neighbors—except our nation.

If you think our displeasure with "rogue states" might have any underpinning in international law, then you will be disappointed to learn on page 31 that

> We will take the actions necessary to ensure that our

efforts to meet our global security commitments and
protect Americans are not impaired by the potential
for investigations, inquiry, or prosecution by the
International Criminal Court (ICC), whose jurisdic-
tion does not extend to Americans and which we do
not accept.

The rule of law in the world, then, is to be upheld by a
nation that has declared itself to be above the law. A child-
ish hypocrisy here assumes the dignity of a nation's foreign policy. But if we perceive an illegitimacy in the catastrophic weapons and ad-lib warfare of other nations, why
should we not perceive the same illegitimacy in our own?

The contradiction between peace and war implies, of
course, at every point a contradiction between security
and war. We wish, this document says, to be cooperative
with other nations, but the authors seem not to realize
how rigidly our diplomacy and our offers to cooperate
will be qualified by this new threat of overwhelming
force to be used merely at the president's pleasure. We
cannot hope to be secure when our government has
declared, by its announced readiness "to act alone," its
willingness to be everybody's enemy.

III. A further contradiction is that between war
and commerce. This issue arises first of all in
the war economy, which unsurprisingly regards war as a
business and weapons as merchandise. However national-
istic may be the doctrine of the National Security

Strategy, the fact is that the business of warfare and the weapons trade have been thoroughly internationalized. Saddam Hussein possesses weapons of mass destruction, for example, partly because we sold him such weapons and the means of making them back when (madman or not) he was our "friend." But the internationalization of the weapons trade is a result inherent in international trade itself. It is a part of globalization. Mr. Bush's addition of his new National Security Strategy to the previous bipartisan commitment to globalization exposes an American dementia that has not been so plainly displayed before.

The America Whose Business is Business has been internationalizing its economy in haste (for bad reasons, and with little foresight), looking everywhere for "trading partners," cheap labor, and tax shelters. Meanwhile, the America Whose Business is National Defense is withdrawing from the world in haste (for bad reasons, with little foresight), threatening left and right, drawing lines in sand, repudiating agreements, and angering friends. The problem of participating in the global economy for the benefit of Washington's corporate sponsors while maintaining a nationalist belligerence and an isolationist morality calls for superhuman intelligence in the secretary of commerce. The problem of "acting alone" in an international war while maintaining simultaneously our ability to import the foreign goods (for instance, oil) on which we have become even militarily dependent will call, likewise, for overtopping genius in the secretary of defense.

The National Security Strategy devotes a whole chapter to the president's resolve to "ignite a new era of global economic growth through free markets and free trade" (p. 17). But such a project cannot be wedded, even theoretically, to his commitment to a militarist nationalism ever prepared "to act alone." One must wonder when the government's corporate clients will see the contradiction and require the nation to assume a more humble posture in the presence of the global economy.

The conflict in future-abuse between this document and the sales talk of the corporations is stark, and it is pretty absurd. On the one hand, we have the future as a consumer's paradise in which everybody will be able to buy comfort, convenience, and happiness. On the other hand, we have this government's new future in which terrible things are bound to happen if we don't do terrible things in the present—which, of course, will make terrible things even more likely to happen in the future.

After World War II, we hoped the world might be united for the sake of peacemaking. Now the world is being "globalized" for the sake of trade and the so-called free market—for the sake, that is, of plundering human societies and the natural world for cheap labor, cheap energy, and cheap materials. How nations, let alone regions and communities, are to shape and protect themselves within this "global economy" is far from clear. Nor is it clear how the global economy can hope to survive the wars of nations.

If a nation cannot be "good," in any simple or incontestable way, then what can it reasonably be that is better than bad?

A nation can be charitable, as we can say with some confidence, for we need not look beyond our own for an example. Our nation, sometimes, has been charitable toward its own people; it has been kind to the elderly, the sick, the unemployed, and others unable to help themselves. And sometimes it has been charitable toward other nations, as when we helped even our one-time enemies to recover from World War II. But "charity" does not refer only to the institutional or governmental help we give to the "less fortunate." The word means "love." The commandment to "love your enemies" suggests that charity must be without limit; it must include everything. A nation's charity must come from the heart and the imagination of its people. It requires us ultimately to see the world as a community of all the creatures which, to be possessed by any one, must be shared by all.

Perhaps that is only a better way of saying that a nation can be civilized. To be civil is to conduct oneself as a responsible citizen, honoring the lives and the rights of others. Our courts and jails are filled with the uncivil, who have presumed to act alone in their own interest. But incivility is now almost conventionally in business among us.

A nation can be independent, as our founders instructed us. If a nation cannot within reasonable measure be independent, it is hard to see how its existence might be justified. Though independence may at times require some sort of self-defense, it cannot be maintained by defiance of other nations or by making war against them. It can be maintained only by the most practical economic self-reliance. At the very least, a nation should be able sustainably to feed, clothe, and shelter its citizens, using its own sources and by its own work.

And of course that requires a nation to be, in the truest sense, patriotic: Its citizens must love their land with a knowing, intelligent, sustaining, and protective love. They must not, for any price, destroy its beauty, its health, or its productivity. And they must not allow their patriotism to be degraded to a mere loyalty to symbols or any present set of officials.

A nation also can abide under the rule of law. Since the Alien and Sedition Laws of 1798, in times of national stress or emergency there have been arguments for the abridgement of citizenship under the Constitution. But the weakness of those arguments is in their invariable implication that a democracy such as ours can work only in the most favorable circumstances. If constitutional guarantees of rights and immunities cannot be maintained in unfavorable circumstances, what is their point or value? Their value in fact originates in the acknowledgement of their usefulness in the times of greatest difficulty and to those in greatest need, as does the value of international law.

It is impossible to think that constitutional government can be suspended in a time of danger, in deference to the greater "efficiency" of centralized power, and then easily or quickly restored. Efficiency may be a political virtue, but only if strictly limited. Our Constitution, by its separation of powers and its system of checks and balances, acts as a restraint upon efficiency by denying exclusive power to any branch of the government. The logic of governmental efficiency, unchecked, runs straight on, not only to dictatorship, but also to torture, assassination, and other abominations.

Such aims as charity, civility, independence, true patriotism, and lawfulness a nation of imperfect human beings may reasonably adopt as its standards. And we may conclude reasonably, rightly, and with no touch of self-contempt that by those standards we are less charitable, less civil, less independent, less patriotic, and less law-abiding than we might be, and than we need to be. And do these shortcomings relate to the president's perception that we are less secure than we need to be? We would be extremely foolish to suppose otherwise.

One might reasonably assume that a policy of national security would advocate from the start various practical measures to conserve and to use frugally the nation's resources, the objects of this husbandry being a reduction in the nation's dependence on imports and a reduction in the competition between nations for necessary goods. One might reasonably expect the virtues of stewardship, thrift, self-sufficiency, and neighborliness to receive a certain precedence in the advocacy of political leaders. Since the country, to make itself secure, may be required to rely on itself, one might reasonably expect a due concern for the health and longevity of its soils, forests, and watersheds, its natural and its human communities, its domestic economy, and the natural systems on which that economy inescapably depends.

Such a concern could come only from perceiving the contradiction between national security and the present global economy, but there is no such perception in the National Security Strategy. This document, ignoring all conflicts, proposes to go straight ahead with both projects: national security, which it defines forthrightly as isolationist, domineering, and violent; and the global economy, which it defines as international humanitarianism. It does allow that there is a connection between our national security and the economic condition of "the rest of the world" (p. 17), and that the extreme poverty of much of the rest of the world is "neither just nor stable" (p. 21). And of course one can only agree. But the authors assume that economic wrongs can be righted merely by "economic development" and the "free market," that it is the nature of these things to cure poverty, and that they will not be impeded by terrorism or a war against terrorism or a preemptive war for the security of one nation. These are articles of a faith available only to a politically sheltered economic elite.

As for conservation here and elsewhere, the authors provide a list of proposals that is short, vague or ambiguous, incomplete, and rather wildly miscellaneous:

We will incorporate labor and environmental concerns

into U.S. trade negotiations… (p. 19)

We will…expand the sources and types of global energy… (pp. 19-20)

We will…develop cleaner and more energy efficient technologies. (p. 20)

Economic growth should be accompanied by global efforts to *stabilize* [my emphasis] greenhouse gas concentrations… (p. 20)

Our overall objective is to reduce America's greenhouse gas emissions relative to the size of our economy, cutting such emissions per unit of economic activity by 18 percent over the next 10 years… (p. 20)

But the only energy technologies specifically promoted here are those of "clean coal" and nuclear power—for both of which there is a strong corporate advocacy and a strong conservationist criticism or opposition. There is no mention of land loss, of soil erosion, of pollution of land, air, and water, or of the various threats to biological diversity—all problems of generally (and scientifically) recognized gravity.

Agriculture, which is involved with all the problems listed above, and with several others—and which is the economic activity most clearly and directly related to national security, if one grants that we all must eat—

receives such scant and superficial treatment as to amount to a dismissal. The document proposes:

1. "a global effort to address new technology, science, and health regulations that needlessly impede farm exports and improved agriculture" (p. 19). This refers, without saying so, to the growing consumer resistance to genetically modified food. A global effort to overcome this resistance would help, not farmers and not consumers, but global agribusiness corporations such as Monsanto.

2. "transitional safeguards which we have used in the agricultural sector" (p. 19). This refers to government subsidies, which ultimately help the agribusiness corporations, not farmers.

3. promotion of "new technologies, including biotechnology, [which] have enormous potential to improve crop yields in developing countries while using fewer pesticides and less water" (p. 23). This is offered (as usual and questionably) as the solution to hunger, but its immediate benefit would be to the corporate suppliers of the technologies.

This is not an agriculture policy, let alone a national security strategy. It has the blindness, arrogance, and foolishness that are characteristic of top-down thinking by politicians and academic experts, assuming that "improved agriculture" would inevitably be the result of catering to the agribusiness corporations, and that national food security can be achieved merely by going on as before. It does not address any agricultural problem as such, and it ignores the vulnerability of our present food system—dependent as it is on genetically impoverished monocultures, cheap petroleum, cheap long-distance transportation, and cheap farm labor—to many kinds of disruption by "the embittered few," who, in the event of such disruption, could quickly become the embittered many. On eroding, ecologically degraded, increasingly toxic landscapes, worked by failing or subsidy-dependent farmers and by the cheap labor of migrants, we have erected the tottering tower of "agribusiness," which prospers and "feeds the world" (incompletely and temporarily) by undermining its own foundations.

But all our military strength, all our police, all our technologies and strategies of suspicion and surveillance cannot make us secure if we lose our ability to farm, or if we squander our forests, or if we exhaust or poison our water sources.

A policy of preemptive war, which rests, as this one does, on such flimsy domestic underpinnings and on too great a concentration of power in the presidency, obviously risks or invites correction. And, as we know, correction can come by three means:

1. By strenuous public debate. But this requires a strong, independent political opposition, which at present we do not have. The country now contains many individuals and groups seriously troubled by issues of civil rights, food, health, agriculture, economy, peace, and

conservation. These people have much in common, but they have no strong political voice, because few politicians have seen fit to speak for them.

2. By failure, as by some serious disruption of our food or transportation or energy systems. This might cause a serious public debate, which might place us on more stable economic and political footing. But we are a large nation, highly centralized in almost every way, and without much self-sufficiency, either national or regional. Any failure, therefore, will be large and not nearly so easy to correct as to prevent.

3. By citizens' initiative. Responsibilities abandoned by the government properly are assumed by the people. An example of this is the already well-established movement for local economies, typically beginning with food. There is much hope in this effort, provided that it continues to grow. And we have, surviving from the Vietnam War, a surprisingly strong and numerous peace movement. As we learned from the Vietnam experience, the only effective answer to a secretive and unresponsive government is a citizens' revolt. The revolt against the war in Vietnam was nonviolent, effective, and finally successful. Such a correction is better than no correction, but it is far from ideal—far less to be preferred than correction by public debate. A citizens' revolt necessarily comes too late. And if it is not peaceable and responsibly led, it could easily destroy the things it is meant to save.

IV. The present administration has adopted a sort of official Christianity, and it obviously wishes to be regarded as Christian. But "Christian" war has always been a problem, best solved by avoiding any attempt to reconcile policies of national or imperial militarism with anything Christ said or did. The Christian gospel is a summons to peace, calling for justice beyond anger, mercy beyond justice, forgiveness beyond mercy, love beyond forgiveness. It would require a most agile interpreter to justify hatred and war by means of the Gospels, in which we are bidden to love our enemies, bless those who curse us, do good to those who hate us, and pray for those who despise and persecute us.

This peaceability has grown more practical, has gained "survival value," as industrial warfare has developed increasingly catastrophic weapons, which are abominable to our government, so far, only when other governments possess them. But since the end of World War II, when the terrors of industrial warfare had been fully revealed, many people and, by fits and starts, many governments have recognized that peace is not just a desirable condition, as was thought before, but is a practical necessity. It has become less and less thinkable that we might have a living and a livable world, or that we might have livable lives or any lives at all, if we do not make the world capable of peace.

And yet we have not learned to think of peace apart from war. We have received many teachings about peace and peaceability in biblical and other religious traditions, but we have marginalized those teachings, have made them eccentric, in deference to the great norm of violence and conflict. We wait, still, until we face terrifying dangers and the necessity to choose among bad alternatives, and then we think again of peace, and again we fight a war to secure it.

At the end of the war, if we have won it, we declare peace; we congratulate ourselves on our victory; we marvel at the newly-proved efficiency of our latest, most "sophisticated" weapons; we ignore the cost in lives, materials, and property, in suffering and disease, in damage to the natural world; we ignore the inevitable residue of resentment and hatred; and we go on as before, having, as we think, successfully defended our way of life.

That is pretty much the story of our victory in the Gulf War of 1991. In the years between that victory and September 11, 2001, we did not alter our thinking about peace and war—that is, we thought much about war and little about peace; we continued to punish the defeated people of Iraq and their children; we made no effort to reduce our dependence on the oil we import from other, potentially belligerent countries; we made no improvement in our charity toward the rest of the world; we made no motion toward greater economic self-reliance; and we continued our extensive and often irreversible damages to our own land. We appear to have assumed merely that our victory confirmed our manifest destiny to be the richest, most powerful, most wasteful

nation in the world. After the catastrophe of September
11, it again became clear to us how good it would be to
be at peace, to have no enemies, to have no more need-
less deaths to mourn. And then, our need for war following with the customary swift and deadly logic our
need for peace, we took up the customary obsession
with the evil of other people.

And now we are stirring up the question whether or
not Islam is a warlike religion, ignoring the question,
much more urgent for us, whether or not Christianity is
a warlike religion. There is no hope in this. Islam,
Judaism, Christianity—all have been warlike religions. All
have tried to make peace and rid the world of evil by
fighting wars. This has not worked. It is never going to
work. The failure belongs inescapably to all of these religions insofar as they have been warlike, and to acknowl-
edge this failure is the duty of all of them. It is the duty
of all of them to see that it is wrong to destroy the
world, or risk destroying it, to get rid of its evil.

It is useless to try to adjudicate a long-standing ani-
mosity by asking who started it or who is the most
wrong. The only sufficient answer is to give up the ani-
mosity and try forgiveness, to try to love our enemies
and to talk to them and (if we pray) to pray for them. If
we can't do any of that, then we must begin again by
trying to imagine our enemies' children who, like our
children, are in mortal danger because of enmity that
they did not cause.

We can no longer afford to confuse peaceability with

passivity. Authentic peace is no more passive than war. Like war, it calls for discipline and intelligence and strength of character, though it calls also for higher principles and aims. If we are serious about peace, then we must work for it as ardently, seriously, continuously, carefully, and bravely as we have ever prepared for war.

When Compassion Becomes Dissent
by David James Duncan

I . I have been serving my country, this deceptively serene Rocky Mountain autumn, as a visiting instructor of creative writing at the University of Montana. I lead two classes, each three hours long, with twenty students all told. My students are not "aspiring writers" exactly: they're the real thing, and in two months' time their collective intensity, wit, and talent have lifted our joint undertaking into the realm of arduous but steady pleasure. Yet as the semester unfolds and we listen to President Bush and his various goaders and backers wage a rhetorical war on Iraq and prepare an increasingly vague national "We" to lay waste to Saddam Hussein possibly, and to civilians and children inevitably, the teaching of creative writing has come to feel, for the first time in my life, like a dissident line of work.

Creative writing requires a dual love of language and of life, human and otherwise. The storyteller then sculpts these raw loves with acute observation, reflection, creative struggle, allegiance to truth, merciless awareness of the foibles of human beings, and unstinting empathy toward human beings even so. Not only have these strategies floundered in the post-9/11 rhetoric and actions of the Bush Administration, they look to me to have been outlawed by two recent federal documents: the 2002 *National Security Strategy of the United States of America* and the 107th Congress's Patriot Act. Had I been invited to proofread these puffed-up rhetorical works with the same critical eye I am paid to apply to student rough drafts, I'd have been forced to tell their authors that they had composed two half-truth-telling, hypocrisy-laden pieces of sociopathic cant and that they should throw them away and start over. Both works redefine Earth as a heavenly body whose countries and cultures the Bush Administration and Congress were appointed to judge and police. Both are based on the belief that opposing Bush rhetoric is traitorous, that spying on neighbors and friends is patriotic, that fighting for our personal freedom "obstructs enhanced surveillance procedures," that weapons of destruction are our greatest protection against weapons of destruction, that terrorizing the citizens of other nations is the greatest safeguard against terrorist acts against our own nation, that biological health, a sustainable natural economy, and the conservation of ecosystems are beneath consideration in this time of red, white, and blue crisis, and that a daily life of compassion and self-examination is the naïve position of sentimentalists and weaklings.

In such an America the teaching of creative writing is one of countless professions that have been inadvertently redefined as dissident. This puts me in an odd position. Having signed a contract to teach before the new Bush/Cheney/Powell "America" existed, and knowing only the former America's literary methods, I'm left no choice but to instruct my students in how to become what the new national lexicon might call "better unAmericans."

2. Another example of how literature has been forced into a dissident position is Bush's presumption (stated in the National Security Strategy on page 5) that it is America's "clear responsibility to history" to "rid the world of evil." As a lifelong student of the world's wisdom literature, it is my duty to inform students that "ridding the world of evil" is a goal very different from any recommended by Jesus, Buddha, or Muhammad, though not so different from some recommended by the Josephs Stalin and McCarthy and by Mao Tse Tung. In wisdom literature the principle evil to be attacked by the person of faith is the evil in oneself, and a secondary evil to be opposed is the power of anyone who victimizes the weak. The National Security Strategy, on the other hand, is a call for unquestioning obedience to and financial support of the Bush Administration's desire to commit our bodies, minds,

ravaged ecosystems, work force, and soldiers to an unspecified series of international bullying actions. Regardless of what we think of this as "patriots," those of us who maintain a politically unfashionable love for the world's scriptures can't help but notice that this document is a hell of a step down in the canon of literature by which people of faith direct their lives.

Another bone I must pick with Bush's aim to "rid the world of evil" is with its authorship. As a novelist, I daily concoct speeches destined to emerge from the mouths of fictitious characters. This practice compels me to point out that, every time he speaks formally (which is to say, reads), the president is a fictitious construct pretending to think thoughts placed in his mouth by others. Thus we see, for example, Bush confusing the words "region" and "regime" as he stands before the United Nations pretending to think thoughts that necessitate war. I'm not making fun of these stumbles. It must be hard to enunciate or understand a daily stream of words you have not written, creatively struggled with, or reflected upon prior to pretending, with the world watching, to think them. The good thing about this lack of authenticity is that Bush may not be such a fool as to believe he can "rid the world of evil;" the horrific thing about it is that our military might and foreign policy are being deployed as if he can. This massive pretense does not imply that Bush is a liar. It implies, far more seriously, that the U.S. presidency itself has become a pretense, hence a lie.

This brings me back to the impossibility of teaching creative writing under the pretentious new National Security Strategy without seeming dissident. As a voluntary professional fiction writer and involuntary amateur liar, I'm here to tell you that fiction-making and lying are two different things. To write *War and Peace* required imaginative effort. To embezzle money from a bank does, too. It should not be necessary to explain even to Jesse Helms that this does not make Tolstoy a bank robber. *War and Peace* is an imaginative invention but also, from beginning to end, a truth-telling and a gift-giving. We know before reading a sentence that Tolstoy "made it all up," but this making is as altruistic and disciplined as the engineering of a cathedral. It uses mastery of language, spectacular acts of empathy, and meticulous insight into a web of individuals and a world to present a man's vast, haunted love for his Russian people. And we as readers get to recreate this love in ourselves. We get to reenter the cathedral.

A lie is also an imaginative invention, but only on the part of the liar. In hearing a lie we can't share in its creativity. Only the liar knows he's lying. The only "gift" a lie therefore gives anyone is belief in something that doesn't exist. This is the cruelty of all lies. There is no corresponding cruelty in fiction. To lie is to place upon the tongue, page, or TV screen words designed to suppress or distort the truth, usually for the sake of some self-serving agenda.

I fear the Bush Administration's claim that Iraq must

be attacked, defeated, and occupied for America's domestic safety is just such a distortion, and that its self-serving aim is the embezzlement not of cash but of Iraq's oil reserves—the second largest on earth. I hope to heaven I'm wrong, but the $73 million Dick Cheney's cohorts at Halliburton have recently invested in oil infrastructure in Iraq despite the presence of Saddam casts a hell of a shadow over my hope, as do the words of Senator Richard Lugar (R., Indiana) of the Senate Foreign Relations Committee, who during the July/August 2002 hearings on Iraq said, "We are going to run the oil business, we are going to run it well, we are going to make money, and it's going to help pay for the rehabilitation of Iraq because there is money there!"

3. The Bush/Cheney/Powell National Security Strategy and Congressional Patriot Act present us with a daily choice between "unpatriotically" serving living beings, the Earth, and international goodwill or "patriotically" serving the corporate nation-state as it transforms our military into a global police force, the world into a police state, and Iraq into an oil-producing colony for "us" and an internment camp for its own people. Post-9/11 anti-Saddam talk has usurped thought, annihilated international trust, and polarized our populace. It has endangered Americans abroad and at home. It has led us further and further from reason, history, and physical reality.

Iraq is not Saddam Hussein. It is the cradle of civilization between the Tigris and Euphrates Rivers, home of the Sumerians and ancient Babylonia, of *The Epic of Gilgamesh*, of Bedouin tribes. Iraq is *Mesopotamia*, for Christ's sake, and the 944,000 cigar-sized depleted uranium (DU)-coated bullets we fired and abandoned there during the Gulf War will remain radioactive roughly one million times longer than all the centuries since ancient Mesopotamia was born. Leukemia and other cancers have ballooned since DU arrived. Military spokespersons scoff the coincidence, claiming that DU radiation can be blocked by a sheet of paper. I know of no man, woman, or child with a sheet of paper located between their mouth and stomach, or between their nostrils and lungs.

Iraq is not Saddam. It is twenty-two million egregiously sanctioned people, fifty-five percent of whom now live in poverty, with a growing majority of children now unschooled because of societal breakdown. Millions of Iraqis are chronically malnourished — a condition permanently damaging to children. U.S. pundits who've never seen Iraq praise the U.N. Oil for Food program as the solution to this problem and blame the ever-handy Saddam for the program's failures. But two successive Oil for Food head coordinators, Denis Halliday and Hans von Sponeck, resigned in protest over the program's insufficiencies and now travel the world preaching that malnutrition remains rampant, and that U.S. political manipulation of the sanctions is the greatest cause of the humanitarian crisis in Iraq. A word from that troublesome old moralist, Leo Tolstoy, seems to be in order: "I sit on a man's back, choking him and making him carry me, and yet assure myself and others that I am very sorry for him and wish to ease his lot by all possible means—except by getting off his back."

4. There is a superstition—fed most savagely these days by corporate thinkers, politicians, and news media—holding that what we hear firsthand is "true" or "real" and that what we merely imagine is "untrue" or "unreal." News reports on what the president said about Saddam today, for instance, are real, while the works of Tolstoy are not. This is nonsense. Insofar as literature enlivens imaginations, firms our grasp of reality, or strengthens our regard for fellow humans, it serves the world. And insofar as the president-character speaks scripts that deny life-threatening facts or erode the careful distinctions that sustain civil discourse and international goodwill, the "real" news report merely disseminates propaganda.

Reportage can, and daily does, lie. Even firsthand experience can lie. And "mere" imaginary experience can open us to truths that would remain inaccessible forever if we had to wait for reportage or experience to teach us the same truth. One of the greatest of human traits, for example, is *compassion*, which means, literally, "to suffer with another." But this high art is seldom born in an instant thanks to "news" or to firsthand experiences. More often its seed is sown via a preliminary magic known as empathy. And empathy begins with a fictive act:

What would it be like to be that black girl four rows in front of me? a little white girl wonders in school one morning. Her imagination sets to work, creating unwritten fiction. In her mind she becomes the black girl, dons her clothes, accent, skin, joins her friends after school, goes home to her family, lives that life. No firsthand experience is taking place. Nothing newsworthy is happening. Yet a white-girl-turned-fictitiously black is linking skin hue to life, skin hue to choice of friends and neighborhood, skin hue to opportunity and history. Words she used without thinking—*African, color, white*—feel suddenly different. And when her imaginary game is over they still sound different. Via sheer fiction, empathy enters a human heart.

To be a Christian, a Buddhist, a Muslim, is to immerse oneself in unstinting fiction-making. Christ's words "Love thy neighbor as thyself," to cite a famously ignored example, demand an arduous imaginative act. This deceptively simple line orders me, as I look at you, to imagine that I am seeing not you, but me, and then to treat this imaginative me, alias you, as if you are me. And for how long? *Till the day I die!* Christ orders anyone who's serious about him to commit the "Neighbor = Me" fiction until they forget for good which of the two of themselves to cheat in a business deal or abandon in a crisis or smart-bomb in a war—at which point their imaginative act, their *fiction-making*, will have turned Christ's bizarre words into a reality and they'll be saying with Mother Teresa, "I see Christ in every woman and man."

Mahatma Gandhi insisted that he was a Christian *and* a Hindu *and* a Muslim *and* a Jew. He also blessed, while dying, the Hindu fanatic who murdered him. In the Middle East, the Balkans, Pakistan, India, New York, Bali, we begin to see why. True, the ability to love neighbor as self is beyond the reach of most people. But the attempt to *imagine* thy neighbor as thyself is the daily work of every literary writer and reader I know. Literature's sometimes troubling, sometimes hilarious depictions of those annoying buffoons, our neighbors, may be the greatest gift we writers give the world when they become warm-up exercises for the leap toward actually *loving* them. Ernest Hemingway made a wonderful statement about this. "Make it up so truly," he advised, "that later it will happen that way." This is, I dare say, Christ-like advice, not just to those practicing an art form known as fiction writing, but to anyone trying to live a faith, defend the weak, or love a neighbor.

5. It is my best guess, this fifteenth day of November 2002, that the civic grief I'm feeling and words I'm setting down will change nothing in the visible world. Americans in power, through a torrent of anti-literature, have turned twenty-two million of our Iraqi neighbors into a single psycho-pathic monster. Though I pray I'm wrong, and thank the international community for opposing the will of

Bush/Cheney/Powell, I still fear that the U.S. may go to war soon, that this war will be brief but devastating, that many more children and civilians will die, that we will never be told their numbers, just as we were not told the numbers killed in Afghanistan or in the Gulf War, and that many Americans for this reason will pretend that no such dead exist. I fear that weapons of mass destruction will be discovered in Iraq, that this discovery will be hailed as the greatest victory yet in "the war against terror," and that the U.S. will use this victory to justify occupying Iraq with a military force whose job it will be to cultivate international goodwill and protect us here at home by brandishing weapons of destruction all day every day at Muslims forbidden to brandish their own. I fear that as we shed more red liquid to ensure a flow of black liquid back to the United States, we will go on fighting for "homeland security," as we have for three years, by cutting funding to Superfund sites, prying open protected lands to industry, hamstringing laws created to protect vanishing species, reducing safeguards against pollutants, defying the Kyoto Accord, assisting in the corporate copyrighting of Earth's plant and animal species and of America's fresh water, curtailing civil liberties, diverting money from education and human resources, excluding biologists, ecologists, humanitarians, and other voices of compassion and science from policy-making groups ruled by private business and greed, stonewalling clean energy tax breaks and legislation, and ignoring sustainable energy technologies that could prevent future oil wars. I fear these courses of action will lead to ever greater addiction to oil, ever more vicious foreign policy, ever more military actions, hence an ever-more-burning desire on the part of the world's disenfranchised to commit acts of violence against us. I pray no such acts occur, though they already have. I pray the next such act will not involve biochemical or nuclear weapons, though we lead the world in the ownership of both. I pray, I pray, I pray. But the only way I know to pluck from the hearts of enemies their desire to destroy us is to remove from their lives the sense that, for their own physical and spiritual survival, they must.

This work will require tens of thousands of acts of atonement. Attempting one such act myself, I last year published two essays expressing my incredulity and grief over the U.S. destruction of Iraq's 1,400 water supply and sewage treatment plants. This destruction took place in defiance of the Geneva Convention. Worse still, our Defense Intelligence Agency (DIA) predicted, in 1991 documents declassified in 2001, that the destruction of these systems would probably not harm Saddam and his army, but *would* lead to epidemic disease, especially among children. The documents go into surprising detail: they note that Iraq's rivers contain biota and pollutants that, unless treated with chlorine, cause cholera, hepatitis, typhoid, and other diseases. They warn that chlorine was embargoed by the sanctions, as were medicines that treat such diseases. Knowing all this, the first Bush Administration destroyed Iraq's clean water anyway.

300,000 tons of raw sewage began to flow daily into Iraq's rivers. The sanctions on chlorine and medicine remained in place.

The DIA documents continued: they mentioned epidemic outbreaks of acute diarrhea, dysentery, respiratory ailments, measles, diphtheria, meningitis, and hepatitis B, causing problems—most notably death—in children. They describe a refugee camp in which four fifths of the population came down with such diseases: eighty percent of the resulting dead were children. When a team of Harvard physicians witnessed the epidemics in the mid-1990s and urged that sanctions barring medicine be lifted, the DIA said the Iraqi regime was exaggerating the incidence of disease and death for political purposes.

This argument against mercy remains in place to this day. A now-world-famous UNICEF study estimates that 500,000 Iraqi children age five and under have died as a result of the combination of sanctions and fouled water.

6. By the time I found and cited the UNICEF study, I knew that many Americans had written it off as "flawed." I therefore set out, with the help of an Internet-deft, altruistic (and Republican) scholar, to research the pros and cons of the study. I learned that the debate over the "500,000" number is the result of understandable confusion: the same number comes from two different sources. The first was a five-day, Iraq-controlled 1995 study of 693 households in Baghdad alone—a study so shoddy that its conclusions were later withdrawn by its

own authors. Its estimate of half a million "excess child deaths" due to U.N. sanctions became famous anyway, thanks to a 1996 Leslie Stahl *60 Minutes* interview of then-Secretary of State Madeleine Albright. When Stahl mentioned the flawed study's "500,000 dead," then asked Albright if the sanctions were still worth it, Albright made the double mistake of responding as if the number was fact, and of answering yes. The number was then pounced upon and often exaggerated by humanitarians, inspiring what one might call "counter-humanitarians" to claim in magazines as diverse as *The New Republic, Commonweal,* and *National Review* that the number is "in dispute" or "leftist whining," and that all blame for the deaths, whatever the number, should be placed not on sanctions but on Saddam.

There are two problems with these counterclaims. The first is that, regardless of the precise number of dead, it is the first Bush Administration, not Saddam's regime, that blew up Iraq's water treatment facilities—and not as an act of war but as a carefully researched act that predicted the ravaging of civilians and children. The second problem with the counterclaims is the 1999 child mortality study done by UNICEF.

Based on interviews conducted in no less than 40,000 Iraqi households—with local assistance but conducted with UNICEF involvement at every stage and technical support from the World Health Organization and independent analysts—this study too concludes that 500,000 more Iraqi children than would have otherwise died in the 1990s, died before reaching the age of five. To greet this finding with politically motivated denials requires an ostrich-lengthed neck and a lot of deep soft sand. The report has been dissected repeatedly. The best such analysis I've found, done by Richard Garfield in 1999, pares away numbers arrived at by shaky data but still concludes that between 1991 and 1998 there was a "likely sum" of 350,000 excess five-and-under child deaths in Iraq, that these deaths are "the tip of the iceberg among damages" yet to occur, that this disaster far exceeds any level of "acceptable damages according to the principles...used in warfare," and that "sanctions and regulations should be modified immediately."

When I first read the UNICEF study my wife and I happened to be nursing our daughters through illnesses that without antibiotics could have killed them both. The number 500,000 destroyed me. The number 350,000 has not brought relief. When I am deeply troubled I fall back on a few trusted mentors. An Indian mentor named Eruch once said, "If you don't know how to take something, take it on the physical level." The closest I can come to following this advice, with regard to the plight of Iraq's children, is to rely on the physical senses, eyes, and heart of a woman named Gerri Haynes.

7. Gerri is a Woodinville, Washington, nurse who heads a group called Washington Physicians for Social Responsibility. She had already been on three missions of mercy to Iraq when, after reading my

OrionOnline essay, "A Prayer for Water and Children," she invited me to join her on a fourth in May of 2002. She was not good at selling her proposal. "It will be sad," she promised. I was unable to join her in part out of fear, in part due to other commitments. But in September 2002 I telephoned Gerri, and we talked for hours about her four journeys.

The first thing that struck me about Gerri Haynes was how respectful she is toward those who've not been hearing about the kinds of things she has seen. "The psyche wants balance," she told me. "It doesn't want a sudden shocking awareness of things that would compel us to change our lives.... In Iraq, children we saw everywhere had the distended bellies of the chronically malnourished. Twelve-year-olds looked like eight-year-olds.... An already burdened person can hardly bear (such) news. Most Americans are kind-hearted. The plain sight of suffering and dying children would inspire almost any of them to realign their lives, change their work, their habits, their thinking, anything, if they saw they were contributing to thousands of children's demise. It's very, very hard to hear this kind of thing."

I told Gerri that in the face of such nightmares I try to console myself with the fact that I am not the "We" who commits military and foreign policy atrocities. Very quietly, Gerri replied, "But we pay taxes. So we fund these disasters. And it's a bipartisan effort. The Clinton Administration was terrible about this. It's not a party-specific problem. This is a government run, in both parties, by greed and multinational interests, a government that wants nothing to do with true humanitarian aims.... Human beings are all made of the same delicate fabric. That's where my 'We' comes from."

My small consolation vanished.

We spoke of the 1999 UNICEF child mortality studies. Gerri's take: "The numbers vary widely, from somewhere around 300,000 to a high of maybe two million. Physicians in Baghdad, when I was there in '99, estimated that 100 to 150 kids were dying just there, every day. But it's a number that's impossible to prove for several reasons. One is that the mechanisms Iraqis had for gathering statistics have not been put back together since the Gulf War. Another is that, after it became apparent that there were limited drugs in the hospitals, many Iraqis stopped bringing their very sick children in. This was particularly true in Basra, where there's a large Bedouin population. These people just keep their kids home, and bury them at home. Gathering exact statistics is impossible.

"We do know that the level of leukemia is greatly increased. We know that congenital malformation has greatly increased. In May 2002 we talked with a woman scientist, Souad Al Azzawi, who said that if the rise in leukemia had been due, as some U.S. politicians claim, to burning oil fires, the pollutants that have since cleared from the environment would have caused the number of leukemia cases to come down. Instead, leukemia levels began to rise five to seven years after 1991—the expected time frame following radiation exposure—and have remained inordinately high. Many believe the answer is DU."

I was impressed that Gerri did not accuse. She just said, "many believe."

"But this doesn't say anything," she added, "to the experience of going to hospital after hospital and seeing every bed with a child in it, sometimes two children per bed— children that look to my eye as though they're very close to death. It doesn't speak to the experience of watching mothers and fathers feel hopeless and helpless to save their children. We *live* on hope. How can we not tell other Americans about what we have participated in creating?"

In 2000, shortly before a planned fourth trip to Iraq, Gerri Haynes was diagnosed with breast cancer. When she mentioned this during our interview I was already so undone by all she'd been saying that I lacked the good grace to ask what she'd been through, or what her prognosis was. I only know that, whatever she endured that year, in September 2001 she was prepared to lead another humanitarian group to Iraq. Then 9/11 happened.

She said, "The delegation had to wait for travel to again become possible. Then they had to try to reorganize. It was difficult. It's very expensive to go there. And time-consuming for people who have full time jobs— people who are using their vacation time to do this arduous, upsetting work."

But in May 2002, Gerri returned to Iraq yet again.

Before this recent trip—amid all the American flag-waving and war-rumblings—Gerri's oldest daughter tried to persuade her to stay home. Gerri didn't describe their discussion, but she did say that, after finally accepting Gerri's sense of mission, daughter offered mother an old-souled piece of advice. "If you do go," she said, "be completely present, wherever you go."

These words returned to Gerri in an Iraqi hospital virtually bereft of medicine and hope. While her group moved from bed to bed, Gerri approached a woman sitting next to her dying child. Gerri speaks no Arabic. The woman spoke no English. Trying to be "present" anyway, Gerri looked at her child, then at the woman, and placed her right hand over her own heart.

The Iraqi mother placed her right hand over her own heart.

Gerri's eyes and the mother's eyes simultaneously filled with tears.

The hospital was crowded. Gerri's visitation time was short. She started to move to the next bed, but then remembered her daughter's words: *"Completely present…"* She and the mother were already crying, their hands over their hearts. There was nothing Gerri could do, despite her medical training, for the child. "How much more present," she wondered, "is it possible to be?"

She stepped forward anyway. With no plan but vague allegiance to the commandment, *"Completely present,"* the nurse without medicine stepped toward the bed of the dying child and inconsolable mother. She then put both of her hands out, palms up.

The Iraqi mother fell into her arms.

"If only this experience were unique!" Gerri told me. "But I can't tell you, any longer, how many mothers I've now held in this same way."

Her voice grew faint over the phone. I heard: *"...diseases that children would almost never die from in the US..."*

I heard: *"...medicine so basic..."*

Then her voice faded, or maybe I drowned it out. I've never taken interview notes while sobbing before.

8. In 1967, at the height of the Vietnam War, Dr. Martin Luther King Jr. may have felt like a minority of one when he spoke up, at the Riverside Church in New York City, against the flag-wavers and public opinion polls of the day. He still had the courage to say, "A time comes when silence is betrayal. Men do not easily assume the task of opposing their government's policy, especially in time of war. We must speak with all the humility that is appropriate to our limited vision, but we must speak. For we are deeply in need of a new way beyond the darkness so close around us.... We are called upon to speak for the weak, for the voiceless, for the victims of our nation, for those it calls enemy, for no document from human hands can make these humans any less our brothers."

To abandon the words of Dr. King is to let the bullet kill him a second time. I believe, based on his call, that no matter what happens in the next war with Iraq, we lose. We lose because we have already lost. We lost when we flew 110,000 sorties over Iraq in forty-two days,

dropping 88,500 tons of ordnance, more than in all of
World War II, on an unsortable tangle of military instal-
lations, palaces, power plants, communications sites,
mosques, schools, homes, civilians, soldiers in arms, soldiers in retreat, soldiers in postures of surrender, soldiers
too shell-shocked to do anything but stand in the road
and accept annihilation. We lost when we characterized
our slaughter of the retreating Iraqi army as a "turkey
shoot" and the incinerated bodies of fathers and sons as
"crispy critters." We lost when Colin Powell, asked for
the number of Iraqi dead produced by this blitzkrieg,
responded, "Frankly that's a number that doesn't interest
me very much." We lost when the first Bush
Administration researched the destruction of water systems, read predictions of death to children, and destroyed
the systems anyway. We lost when we urged the U.N. to
ban chlorine and medicines, witnessed the ensuing epidemics, and refused to ease the sanctions. We lost when
we scattered tons of depleted uranium dust over Iraq
that will go on assaulting all lifeforms for eons. We lost
when we were apprized of studies showing such cancer
increases as lymphoma (four-fold), lung (five-fold), breast
(six-fold), uterine (nearly ten-fold), skin (eleven-fold),
liver (eleven-fold), ovarian (sixteen-fold), but *still* denied
the connection, still make and deploy DU, and recently
nixed, by pressuring the U.N., a World Health
Organization study of DU in Iraq. We lost when we last
week allocated $355.5 billion toward more such
"defense" activities in 2003. We will go on losing as long

as we go on pretending to prevent evil by inflicting these abysmal "strategies."

There is no man or woman, no nation, no mortal power on Earth capable of "ridding the world of evil" as George W. Bush has vowed to do. The desire is preposterous. To act upon preposterousness with vast military might is evil. To acquiesce in such evil is somnolence.

One and a quarter billion Muslims share this world with us. Bush/Cheney/Powell seem to seek their mass conversion to corporate Texas "values." I seek to remember Gandhi's declaration that he was a Christian, a Hindu, a Muslim, a Jew. I seek Dr. King's sense of brotherhood with people who surrender five times a day "to the Merciful, the Compassionate." I seek, in the face of my own or anyone's failure to live by the Gospels or Koran, to "make it up so truly that later it will happen that way."

To define compassion as dissident does not alter the Compassionate. To define mercy as unpatriotic does not change the eternally Merciful. Gerri Haynes placing her palms out to the mother of a dying child, that mother falling into her arms, their joined tears—this is a victory over evil.

The child died even so.

Jesus. Muhammad. Allah. God. Help our "strategists" and "patriots" make up our neighbors more truly.

APRIL 9, 2003: A POSTSCRIPT

In March 2003 the United States preemptively invaded Iraq, ousted Saddam's regime, and has now committed itself to occupying the country for some time to come. Because this began as a literary essay on the current war against imagination and compassion, I'll try to resist the op-ed urge and confine myself to a few notes in keeping with what I've written:

I. That food, medicine and clean water should soon begin to flow to the Iraqi people is a blessing. But that tens of thousands of women, children, bystanders, journalists and soldiers are dead and wounded, that Iraq is in chaos, that most of the world including some of our staunchest allies have been alienated and the Middle East polarized, that Americans at home and abroad are in greater danger than at any time since World War II, that U.S. weapons makers are thriving on fear and devastation, that a clutch of neoconservatives seem to own the U.S. government and media lock, stock, and barrel, that the Bush Administration continues to be, diplomatically, economically, and environmentally, arguably the most myopic, spendthrift and belligerent in

49

our history, and that the new National Security Stategy calls for further operations akin to the invasion of Iraq, is hard to see as anything but terrifying.

2. Though I live to serve peace, I plead mercy and understanding for U.S. troops. Much of the force fighting this war enlisted after 9/11. Most come from a generation of working poor created by the sinking of the middle class. Most are from a generation of TV-watchers unaware that what now passes for news is a disingenuous edit of reality with a strongly biased agenda. The last thing needed in the beleaguered name of "peace" is to greet these vets in the way so many were greeted upon return from Vietnam. These men and women went to Iraq at the risk of their lives with the thought of "avenging 9/11" as the president recommended. That the president's logic was specious does not negate the soldiers' sacrifice. What's more, the weapons our troops have deployed include bunker bombs and armor-piercing shells coated with DU. Doug Rokke— the physicist responsible for on-the-ground clean-up after the Gulf War—holds DU to be responsible for tens of thousands of cases of Gulf War Syndrone, including his own. In Afghanistan—the last place we used DU— the level of uranium in the general populace has increased 25 times over. Those asking God to protect our troops from enemies might do even better to ask that He protect them from their own radioactive ordnance and the leaders and manufacturers who supply it.

3. While it is not generally deemed treasonable that the U.S. armed Saddam in the first place, or that U.S. weapons makers arm the world to the teeth, or that the CIA, to boost approval for this war, presented the Bush Administration with forged evidence of a nonexistent Iraqi nuclear weapons program and that this evidence was used to sway the people, or that the Bush Administration fought the war to wrest away alleged "weapons of mass destruction" but at the same time stockpiles its own such weapons, or that the U.S. refuses to ratify, support, or sign the Antiballistic Missile Treaty, the Biological and Toxin Weapons Convention, the UN Small Arms Agreement, the International Criminal Court Treaty, the Land Mine Treaty, the Nuclear Test Ban Treaty, or that Bush cronies and corporate policy-makers avail themselves of tax loopholes, evading taxes even as they reap billions in tax rebates, leaving average Americans and future generations to fund the current $2-billion-a-day-military budget and gargantuan national debt, America's neoconservative pundits deem it treason-able to have opposed this war.

4. Yet on February 15th of this year, hundreds of millions of people demonstrated against this war in 600 cities worldwide. What an ocean of self-giv-ing sympathy for the treasonous! The website showing photos of a hundred or so of these massive peace march-es may be the most remarkable thing I've seen on a computer screen.

5. Six hundred cities. Hundreds of nations. Hundreds of millions of people. Yet these marchers earned from George W. Bush the smirking remark, "I don't listen to focus groups." And CNN coverage of the march in Manhattan depicted near-empty streets filmed some time after the event was over. To those shocked by such responses to the greatest anti-war demonstration in the known history of humanity, I recommend another dissident work of literature—Tolkien's *Lord of the Rings*, and specifically, his depiction of the mysterious objects known as *palantiri*. These are the glowing orbs that give the wizard Saruman and the Gondor steward, Denethor, far-ranging visions of what is happening all over Middle Earth. But those visions, while depicting actual events, are secretly controlled by the Dark Lord of Mordor, and so cause Saruman to turn to the service of darkness and Denethor to succumb to despair.

American TV news is our contemporary palantir. The kind of work done in Vietnam by journalists such as Peter Arnett and David Halberstam is no longer seen not because it's not being attempted, but because it is no longer allowed on the air. The best investigative journalists I know spurn TV as a source. One such, Richard Manning, calls our current TV news "marvelously clever, and worse than useless. The right has leveraged the key positions of message dissemination. And when you control the propaganda machine, you don't have to govern worth a damn. No matter how bad you blow it, your media machine can keep spinning it." Corporate TV's skewed accounts of "reality" invade and shrivel our imaginations daily. Many suspect this, yet too often accept it, indulge in it, sink into it. Corporate-owned network news is systematically *disheartening*, its influence insidious. In Tolkien's climactic *The Return of the King*, when Denethor is overwhelmed by the power behind the palantir, he cries to Gandalf, "I have seen more than thou knowest, Grey Fool... Thy hope is but ignorance. Go then and labour in healing! Go forth and fight! *Vanity...* Against the Power that now arises there is no victory." He then tries but fails to murder his own wounded son, and burns himself to death in despair.

The DU to which our sons and daughters and all Iraq and Afghanistan is being exposed is murderous, though our palantir refuses to deem it so. And the greatest peace march in world history was not "a focus group," though our palantir showed the president deeming it so. Even despite television, an enormous global movement has been born out of love for the Earth and all life, and loathing for the empowered few's continued abuses against Earth and life. February 15, 2003 let us witness this. I refuse to let the palantir erase it.

One of the ironically sweet fruits of war, or of opposition to it, is friendship. Early this morning I phoned my war-won friend and hero, Nurse Gerri Haynes. When I asked how she was faring, Gerri said she'd just given a talk at Stanford, and hoped to dash off to an airport to greet a nine-year-old Iraqi boy arriving in San Francisco for treatment after being injured during a 1999 sanctions-period U.S. "fly-over" bombing. She then dashed to another airport, flew home to Seattle, and began to host a friend she'd made while doing peace work on the Gaza Strip. Gerri rises at 4:30, she said, "because I'm old but still have a lot to get done!" She had asked me to call at 5:30. Her schedule would soon kill me. All it did to Gerri was give her a frog in her throat that made her sound, despite being a grandma, like an erudite seven-year-old.

When she asked how I was faring, I said I've been chanting two mantras—one from Mother Teresa, who said, *"We can do no great things—only small things, with great love,"* and one from Johnny Wooden, the legendary UCLA basketball coach, who said, "Don't let the things you can't do interfere with the things you can do."

I know of no citizen who worked harder or more lovingly to solve the Iraqi peoples' crisis via peaceable means. So I asked Gerri how she was coping with Iraq's devastation.

She said she felt horrible that we'd chosen war, horrible for our troops and the nightmares they were living, and horrible for her countless friends in Iraq. But balancing that she felt heartened by all that happened before the war. "Never before," she said, "has the legitimacy of war been so vehemently questioned and widely opposed." She also hoped, though guardedly, that for the Iraqi people the worst fears and suffering are over.

I proposed to ask Gerri a single formal interview

question, and to end this postscript with her reply. She promised to disappoint, but invited me to proceed.

I said, "Bill Moyers has said he's never seen American democracy so close to collapse. Peter Matthiessen has said he believes our government just made the biggest blunder in its history. A journalist friend tells me that opponents of this war include former CIA agents and conservative career diplomats who know and worked in the Middle East and are, and I quote, 'scared shitless by this insane idea of sorting through the Islamic world for terrorists and control of oil.' Here in the States the natural economy is crumbling, the money economy is following suit, and historians are calling the split between Bush supporters and opponents the most significant division in our society since the Civil War. This war has been hard on the goodhearted everywhere and has peace activists feeling corraled and silenced. Are you with me so far?"

Gerri said she was.

"Everything I just said was from the perspective of my mind. But now, if you're willing, I'd like us to take a jump into our hearts."

She was willing.

I said, "As bad as things look, as bad as they *are*, I keep thinking about... No, *'thinking'* isn't strong enough. I keep *bowing down to* my best notion of the state that Jesus calls *the peace that passeth understanding*. And my feeling is, this peace is in no way altered. It can't be. It is everywhere in the universe. It pierces and permeates the earth and sky. And it exists in all its fullness even when our countrymen and women, friends, sons, daughters, forego peace and go to war. Would you agree?"

Gerri said she would.

"So," I said, "for the sake of everyone who opposed this war then watched it erupt, everyone who now feels impotent or afraid, I was hoping you'd tell us: How do you stay in touch with this peace, even as we involuntarily fund yet voluntarily resist a leadership that has proven itself violent, nondiplomatic, manipulative, and destructive of life and international trust?"

Without hesitation, Gerri said, "My responsibility to stay in touch with the deep peace you've described is *constant*. If I move outside that peace, if I give way to anger or rage due to what I see as patently wrong, then I have lost touch of my covenant with peacefulness, and with a life promise to be of love."

As goosebumps ran down my spine, Gerri said she hadn't expressed herself very well. I smiled in disagreement, but said, "Then try again."

"It's my experience," she said, "that anger always covers sadness, and that sadness always covers something we're unable to do. So, whenever I feel anger I've trained myself to ask, *What is it that I'm unable to do here?* Usually it's just a matter of finding the thing that's thwarting me, recognizing it, and forgiving it. Like, say you need to get someplace, and you get caught in a traffic snarl. You feel angry. But if you trace your anger back through your sadness, to the snarl, you realize it's not the traffic's fault."

I pictured the TV news as a snarl in the psyche of the American populace, preventing them from reaching and living from their hearts. Gerri said, "I still haven't said it very well." I again disagreed, but said, "Take another whack."

She said, "My work in the world must come from a peaceful core, because that core comes from a deep realization that I am intimately united with all life on Earth, and that God, as I experience God, is love. If we believe that God is love, then anything we do must be *of* love in order to reflect God. This is the standard I use to monitor all my thoughts, my words, and my deeds. Not just my actions. It's a standard I apply to everything."

I found myself thinking of Zoroaster, the earlier prophet of Iran, who preached—and more significantly, *lived*—a simple gospel of "good thoughts, good words, good deeds."

"One of the things I love best about being in the Middle East," Gerri said, "is the call to prayer. The one in the morning silence, especially. You realize, each time you hear it, that everyone else is hearing it, too. And if all of us listeners let it help us be reflective, let it be a call to love, it can really help us get through our day. The call to prayer tells me that the instant I move outside the place of peacefulness, I act out of ego rather than soul, and out comes the ego's fears and its sense of failure. When we act out of love, though, it's often magic, and helps those around us act out of love as well."

Much as I liked hearing this, I felt an urge to challenge

Gerri's discourse, to make things harder. I hoped this urge came of love, wasn't at all sure, but let fly anyhow.

"On my desk," I said, "is a photo you sent me last fall. It's of four Iraqi children—three beaming girls and the top quarter or so of what must be a mischievous little boy, because he's obviously poked his head up into the shot from the side. Your husband took it on the streets of Basra in May 2002. You've met, and tried to serve, thousands of children like these. You and countless others were first barred from serving them by the sanctions, and now are blocked by the war and its aftershocks. Sometimes these past few weeks it's really hurt to look at this photo. Sometimes, seeing the explosions over Baghdad, I just couldn't look. What does this photo, these beautiful faces, make you feel today?"

I could hear a shudder through the phone. When Gerri spoke up again, her exceedingly kind voice had a fierceness I'd not yet heard. "Okay. Okay. *Listen*," she said. "*Here's* how I get through this." She drew a deep breath.

"Every time I feel anger, I close my eyes. And I am immediately on a street in Baghdad, or Basra. Or Mosul—where Nineveh is. Or in some little village, Babylon or Ur. Every time I feel anger or helplessness I close my eyes and go to a place I've been—sometimes a place I'm afraid for, sometimes not—in Iraq, or sometimes Palestine, or Israel. And I just start sending love. It sounds hokey, I know. But it works, it saves me from despair. I try to answer the anger I feel, or the horror at what's happening, by going to a place I remember and sending love to all the life around me.

"Like the Palestine Hotel. You've heard about this? The hotel in Baghdad, where the journalists are staying? U.S. forces shot a rocket into it yesterday. It's where we always stay, a wonderful place—and the staff is so dear! So friendly and kind. So when I remember what's happened and feel what it makes me feel, I close my eyes, go there, and start sending. I see the staff, and send love. Or maybe the fountain across the street, all the people around it. The shoeshine boy, people in the halls, on sidewalks, every face I can remember, all the faces I know. And I just love them as much as I can possibly send love."

Her voice broke on the last few words, but she kept brokenly speaking. "Or sometimes it's the Tigris I send to. How it flows by, needing so badly to be cared for, to be brought back to health, you know what I mean? So I try to wrap my arms around the river, and all its people, and to enclose them in love. I don't think about whether it's working. I don't worry about failure. I just send it, send it, send it."

At the thought of all we've sent instead I felt a hot wash of anger. So I closed my eyes, took a long cool breath, and at once saw the four Basra children in the photo. Knowing Gerri was already sending love, I felt an urge to broaden our collective giving. So, as much as I possibly could, I sent knowledge of safe places to hide. I sent a quick end to the war. I sent a Tigris so clean there were trout in the clear Kurdish headwaters, and sent forgiveness to the Kurds who lived beside the trout. I sent

calm to the hearts of the marines who fear every mov-
ing Iraqi car. I sent an army of altruists armed with
Geiger vacuums capable of sucking DU out of soil and
streets and air. I sent the deep peace I have sensed almost
everywhere but through the palantir and in the minds of
the greed- and hate-driven—the peace a diverse and
loving new humanity stands ready to serve. It sounds
hokey, like Gerri said. There will be decades of solid
work, centuries of solid work, to be done in the wake of
all this. But even in this time of war on the imagination,
the body wants to follow where free imaginations lead.
In our moment of seeming helplessness, our sending
helps save us.

Acknowledgments

The Orion Society would like to thank the Ruth Brown Foundation, David Rosenstein, and the many other contributors to Orion's Thoughts on America Initiative for their generous support of this book, especially Agnes Gund and Daniel Shapiro, George and Trudy Dittmar, Deborah Reich, Elizabeth Jennings, David Orr and the Compton Foundation, Liese Keon, Pamela Johnston, Peter Schuyler, Louis Casimir, Cathy Weiss and the Claneil Foundation, John McClenahan, and John R. and Barbara K. Newsom. For more information on the Thoughts on America Initiative, visit www.oriononline.org or call 888/909-6568.

About the Authors

Wendell Berry, farmer, essayist, poet and novelist, is the author of more than thirty books including, *In the Presence of Fear: Three Essays for a Changed World*. This essay, an abridged version of one appearing in *Orion* Magazine, was printed as a full-page statement in The New York Times on February 9, 2003, as part of The Orion Society's Thoughts on America Initiative.

David James Duncan is the author of the novels *The River Why* and *The Brothers K*, and a collection of memoir and stories, *River Teeth*. His most recent book, *My Story as Told by Water*, won the Western States Book Award and was nominated for the 2001 National Book Award.

The Orion Society

The Orion Society's mission is to inform, inspire, and engage individuals and grassroots organizations across North America in becoming a significant cultural force for healing nature and community. Our programs and publications include:

***Orion* Magazine:** Since 1982, *Orion* has worked to reconnect human culture with the natural world, blending scientific thinking with the arts, engaging the heart and mind, and striving to make clear what we all have in common.

Orion publishes the work of the writers who are shaping a relationship between nature and a new emerging cultural ethic—Barbara Kingsolver, Gary Paul Nabhan, Sandra Steingraber, David Quammen,

Richard Nelson, Terry Tempest Williams, Barry Lopez, Robert Michael Pyle, Thomas Moore, David James Duncan, Wendell Berry, Scott Russell Sanders, Ann Zwinger—as well many new voices.

Orion also includes powerful visual images that blur the boundaries between the human and the natural, and challenge us to see our world from new perspectives. Each issue includes portfolios of paintings and photographs from artists such as Frans Lanting, Galen Rowell, Sonya Bullaty, Wolf Kahn, Forrest Moses, and Andy Goldsworthy.

OrionOnline.org: Orion's website features powerful and poignant multimedia content, including web-exclusive articles, videos, and art exhibitions, which are publicized via our popular e-mail updates.

Orion Books: Orion's books range from the popular Nature Literacy Series of educational resources to the New Patriotism Series of essays.

Orion Grassroots Network: The Network encompasses over 500 organizations, diverse in their focus and locale, that are dedicated to healing our fractured relationships with nature and community. To nurture these groups, the Orion Grassroots Network offers a number of strategically created services to ease the isolation of working issue-by-issue by providing a forum where they experience their work as part of the broad movement for cultural change. To learn more: www.oriononline.org/ogn.

The Orion Society is a 501(c)3 nonprofit organization.

Learn more about *Orion*, or purchase additional copies of *Citizens Dissent* or any of our other publications at **www.oriononline.org**.

For information on bulk or wholesale orders of *Citizens Dissent*, or any of our other publications, please call 888/909-6568.

The Orion Society
187 Main Street, Great Barrington, MA 01230
telephone: 413/528-4422   facsimile: 413/528-0676
email: orion@orionsociety.org   website: www.oriononline.org

Also available in this series

Volume 1

In the Presence of Fear
Three Essays for a Changed World

by Wendell Berry

i. Thoughts in the Presence of Fear
ii. The Idea of a Local Economy
iii. In Distrust of Movements

ISBN 0-913098-60-4
Paperback, 64 pages, $8.00

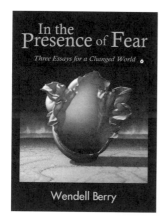

In these three poignant essays, author Wendell Berry reflects deeply on the current sources of world hope and despair.

Berry's powerful "Thoughts in the Presence of Fear," written for OrionOnline in response to the September 11 attacks on New York and Washington D.C., together with two related essays previously published in *Orion* magazine, provide a much needed roadmap for healing our communities and guiding us as just and responsible citizens.

Order online, at www.OrionOnline.org, or by calling toll-free, 888/909-6568. Bulk and wholesale pricing is available.

Volume 2

Patriotism and the American Land

by Richard Nelson, Barry Lopez,
and Terry Tempest Williams

ISBN 0-913098-61-2
Paperback, 88 pages, $8.00

Terrorism. Homeland Security. Patriotism. Since September 11, 2001, these terms have emerged as a fundamental part of our cultural lexicon, with their unsaid assumptions and attendant emotions being used to inspire and buttress a varied set of cultural, political, and military responses to the events of that tragic day.

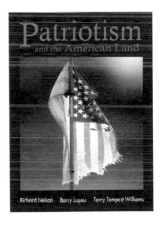

In the months since that seminal moment in our nation's history, like most Americans we have been deeply immersed in a process of reflection and an ongoing review of the words and actions of our leaders, our media, and our fellow citizens. On numerous occasions and in different contexts we have been moved to ask the following questions. What is terrorism? What does a secure homeland really look like? Who is a patriot? The three essays in *Patriotism and the American Land* attempt to address these questions.

A Citizen's Response to the National Security Strategy of the United States of America Poster

Presented in The New York Times on February 9, 2003

On February 9, 2003, The Orion Society's Thoughts on America Initiative placed a full-page statement in Section A of the Sunday New York Times. The "OpAd" was an abridged version of the cover article for the March/April 2003 issue of Orion magazine, "A Citizen's Response to the National Security Strategy of the United States of America," by Wendell Berry. The Times statement garnered a great deal of attention around the world and inspired many of the millions of people who turned out later that week to protest the American policies in Iraq. A series of similar ads on topics relating to America's position in, and relation to, the world are planned throughout the country. The poster measures 18x24 and is printed in full color.